Baptism of The Holy Ghost

by

W.B. Godbey

First Fruits Press
Wilmore,
Kentucky
c2018

Baptism of the Holy Ghost.
By W.B. Godbey.
First Fruits Press, © 2018

ISBN: 9781621718277 (print), 9781621718284 (digital), 9781621718291 (kindle)

Digital version at https://place.asburyseminary.edu/godbey/20/

For all other uses, contact:

First Fruits Press
B.L. Fisher Library
Asbury Theological Seminary
204 N. Lexington Ave.
Wilmore, KY 40390
http://place.asburyseminary.edu/firstfruits

Godbey, W. B. (William Baxter), 1833-1920.
    Baptism of the Holy Ghost / by W.B. Godbey. – Wilmore, KY : First Fruits Press, ©2018.

    pages ; cm.

    Reprint. Previously published: Greensboro, N.C. : Apostolic Messenger Office, [190-?]
    ISBN: 9781621718277 (pbk.)
    1. Baptism in the Holy Spirit.   I. Title.

BT123.G622 2018

Cover design by Jon Ramsay

asburyseminary.edu
800.2ASBURY
204 North Lexington Avenue
Wilmore, Kentucky 40390

First Fruits
THE ACADEMIC OPEN PRESS OF ASBURY SEMINARY

First Fruits Press
The Academic Open Press of Asbury Theological Seminary
204 N. Lexington Ave., Wilmore, KY 40390
859-858-2236
first.fruits@asburyseminary.edu
asbury.to/firstfruits

Baptism of the Holy Ghost

By

W. B. Godbey

AUTHOR OF
"New Testament Commentaries." "New Testament
Translation," and a great number of
other books and booklets.

Published by the

APOSTOLIC MESSENGER OFFICE

900 Silver Run Ave.
Greensboro, N. C.

Four hundred years have rolled away since God had said a word to Israel through an inspired prophet; so many having come in by-gone ages that the country seemed to be literally enchanted with them; their hallowed memories still lingering; their footprints still visible.

It truly seemed to Israel that God had forsaken her and left her to float **ad libitum** on the sea of time, taking chances with the whole Gentile world for a happy landing.

Therefore, the rise of John the Baptist, not only an inspired prophet, but the greatest prophet who had ever trodden the globe; aye, more than a prophet, because he was precursor and honored introducer of his Lord. He began to preach in the wilderness where, in the providence of God, he was brought, [because Herod's soldiers were massacreing all the male infants two years old and younger in and about Bethlehem, in order to be sure to get Jesus; though there was no such an order given for Juttah, yet Zechariah and Elizabeth, zealous for the safety of their son, migrated away to the wilderness of Judea and never returned.] Therefore when John reached majority—thirty years—he persued to Levitical law, began to preach in the wilderness.

(a) John was really so identical in his ministerial character with Elijah the prophet, that inspiration cognomened him the Elijah to come.

Elijah's prophetical life was all spent in an arduous and faithful ministry to restore the law, which God had given them through Moses on Mt. Sinai, for all Israel. John was the successor of Elijah in the fact that he came to finish the work in which Elijah had spent his life. His preaching was unscathed lightning from a clouded sky; so incisive and penetrating that none could resist it; all went down before it, repenting in dust and ashes. Every one that heard him, ran away and told every one that he met, the news that there was a wonderful prophet preaching in the wilderness of Judea. Consequently all who heard of him dropped everything and put out to see for themselves. Soon the road leading into the wilderness was flooded with people—all classes: the rich on their camels; the middle classes on donkeys, and the poor trudging along through the dust with their dogs—all pressing their way into the wilderness, the eager throng hanging spellbound on the eloquent lips of the paradoxical prophet.

Meanwhile there was but one voice ringing from every lip: "Surely this one is the Christ of God, the Shiloh of prophecy and the Savior of the world." Priests are seen with the long roll of prophecies out before their eyes and searching diligently to see if he does verify the prophetical character of the Christhood. In Their enthusiasm to solve the dilemma, they send to him a delegation of priests and Levites publicly to interview him: "Art thou the Christ or do we look for another?" He unhesitatingly answers, "I am not the Christ, but the voice of one roaring in the wilderness, prepare ye the way of the Lord and make His paths straight," i. e.: Repent of all your sins and straighten out everything crooked in your lives, the Christ will not travel a crooked way.

(b) While he positively certifies that he is not the Christ, he procedes to tell them that the Christ is already on the earth and that he has come to reveal Him to them so that there may be no mistake about identity.

Six months have rolled away and early in his ministry he found it necessary to move out of the wilderness to the Jordan. Not as people superstitiously suppose, to get immersion water, as he did not immerse anybody and had already been baptizing them in the wilderness where there is no immersion water, as I have been through there eight times.

"How do you know that John did not immerse?" Because he tells me (Mark 1: 8; Luke 3: 16; Acts 1: 5, 11: 16 and Heb. 10: 22), that he handled the water and not the people. Besides he says he did with the water the very thing that Jesus was going to to do with the Holy Ghost and fire, as he used the same word in both cases to tell what he did with water and what Jesus did with the Holy Ghost and fire. As we know the Holy Ghost and fire fell on them, we know the fire did the same thing as John, Jesus, Paul, Peter, Mark, Luke and Apollos all certify in the citations above mentioned. John moved to the Jordan to accommodate the multitude with plenty of water which they did not have in the wilderness.

(c) The multitudes have wonderfully increased, the people gathered from all parts of the Hebrew world. About ten thousand hanging spellbound on the eloquent lips of the wonderful prophet standing on a rock and the people all around, transported with his stentorious voice, bearing the awful judgment-day truth to their minds.

Meanwhile he suddenly shouts so loud as he points away toward the north, "Behold the Lamb of God that taketh away the sin of the world." All eyes are turned thitherward and stretched wide open, hoping to see the wonderful personage for whom they had been looking all their lives, and especially since the rise of John the Baptist in their midst.

They see Him coming, as He has traveled on foot eighty miles from His humble home in Nazareth, having there waited patiently till he reached His majority and could legally enter upon His official Messiahship.

John, dismounting the rock goes to meet Him. The multitude reverentially crowd together and give them room to pass till they both meet. Oh, what a wonderful meeting! The Son of God, the Savior of the world and the greatest prophet mortal eyes had ever seen, met each other, reminding me of the meeting of Napoleon Bonaparte and the Czar of Russia on a raft in the middle of the River of Tilsit on the border of Russia, amid the roar of artillery on either bank. They were the two most influential men in the world at that time, but how infinitely transcendant the meeting of John the Baptist and the Savior of the world. The latter demanding the baptism of the former—His official introduction into His Mesiah-ship—when John modestly declines, observing, "I have need to be baptized of Thee and comest Thou to me?" Jesus responded, "Suffer it to be so now, as it becometh us to fulfill all righteousness." Then John acquiesced and poured the limpid rill on the head of his Lord as the statuary I saw in catacombs of Rome, representing Jesus standing and John pouring the water on His head. Two years ago I saw in the house of Judas in Damascus where Paul was converted under the ministry of Ananias, who baptized him, the life size statuary of Ananias pouring water on the head of Paul.

Chapter I.

THE BAPTISM OF THE HOLY GHOST NECESSARY IN EVERY CASE

John was filled with the Holy Ghost from the womb of his mother, happily converted under the influence of his saintly father and mother, sanctified before he backslid, receiving it prophetically, like the patriarchs and prophets.

If there ever was a human being who did not need the baptism of the Holy Ghost, John was that one. And still he certifies under the inspiration of the Holy Ghost that he did need it; thus clearly recognizing its indispensability in every case. Oh, how pertinent that every one should recognize that fact and govern themselves accordingly. It is the absolute **sine qua non** of admission into heaven. Oh, how the whole world needs awakening on it.

(d) No wonder Satan turns all the battering rams of the pandemonium against it. If possible to demolish and sweep it from the field. He makes such an awful effort to starve off and eclipse it by substitutes. As the same word in the Bible means the baptism of the Holy Ghost and the baptism of water, he ransacks earth and hell to manipulate water into the substitution of the spirit, which gives him the complete victory, because the water is only the sign, and not the thing itself at all, any more than the shade of a tree is the tree. In that way Satan runs people into foolishness and utterly cheats them out of their souls.

Debating with a Campbellite in Greenville, Tenn., he laid great emphasis on "born of water," as a proof of immersion, ringing changes on the fact that you can't be born of a thing smaller than yourself, and consequently the little sprinkle of the Bible (Ezek. 36:25; Isa. 52:15; Heb. 9:9; 1 Cor. 10 chap.) would not do.

N. B. The inspired writers never made any divisions in chapters. That was done by the London printers, 1551, in order to dispense it to the people, just as you have to cut up a beef to give it out for the people to eat. Now wink at the fourth chapter division of John and you run immediately into His sermon which He preached to the women at Jacob's well, when He mentioned the water seven times, whereas with Nicodemus, only once. The woman thought He meant the water sparkling ninety feet down in Jacob's well, as she had come all the way to get it. But He told her twice over that she was mistaken and He meant Living Water, i. e., the water of life.

Nicodemus made the glaring mistake now characteristic of the Campbellites and Mormons and other materialistic infidels; thinking that Jesus meant His body, observing, "How can a man be born when he is old, can he enter the second time into his mother's womb and be born?" showing positively that he thought our Savior meant an operation to be performed upon his body. But you see that he was glaringly mistaken, as Jesus said, "That which is generated of depravity, is depravity, that which is generated of the spirit, is spirit, marvel not that I said unto you, Ye must be born from above?" Showing clearly the materialistic blunder of Nicodemus and the pure spirituality of the birth here mentioned, having absolutely nothing to do with his body.

How strange that so many people keep tangled up in the materialistic heresy of Nicodemus when they have the positive correction of Jesus right before their eyes.

(e)   Eph. 2:1: "You hath He quickened, who

were dead in trespasses and in sins." The word for quickened there is **zopoicse,** from **zoce,** life, and **poio,** to create; therefore it means to create life in a dead soul. The Holy Ghost is God. When He regenerates a soul, He creates divine life in it. That life is the water and the Holy Ghost the spirit; therefore that soul is born of water and spirit, i. e., born of the divine life and the Holy Spirit, the omnipotent Executative of the new birth.

In a similar manner,, Satan uses his false prophets in an awful effort to actually eclipse the baptism of the Holy Ghost by immersion. As it is so big, it is impossible to receive it without looking at it, and consequently it is so detrimental to spirituality, because if you do not lose sight of everything and take Jesus for everything you need, you will never get the victory. Even after you get it, if you run off after ordinances or anything else you will lose it. Jesus is everything in the plan of salvation. Consequently you must take Him for everything. When you magnify an ordinance, you always minify Christ, and the great tendency to nullify Him, as Campbellites do, actually leave Him out, only recognizing Him as the administrative Agent, whereas He is both. Anything that minifies or nullifies the work of Christ is from the bottomless pit, because the Bible clearly reveals that He is everything. Paul warns us, (Col. 2: 7), "Beware lest any one deceive you and lead you astray, according to vain philosophy and the elements of the world and not according to Christ, for in Him dwelleth all the fulness of the Godhead bodily," i. e., in the body of Christ dwells all the fulness of the Father, Son and Holy Ghost. Hence you see He has everything in Him. "You are complete in Him, who is the head of all principality and power, being circumcised with the circumcision made without hands in putting off the body of carnality by the circumcision of Christ; being buried with Him in baptism." Here you see the thing buried is the carnality which you put off. That word in putting off the body of sin carnality, which is old Adam, here described as an old worn out, stenchy garment, which you put off.

The word translated "putting off," is **apodusie**, a powerful tripple Greek compound from the verb **duo**, to put on as a garment, and **ded**, to put off, and **apo**, which means to throw away. Therefore the word means to put off the old, filthy, stenchy garment and throw it out of your way, i. e., ship it beyond the north pole so it can never get back.

(f) You see here that we get it in baptism, not with water as there is not a drop in a million miles, but the baptism in this passage is here said to be the circumcision made without hands, in putting off the sin of depravity. We get it all in Christ because He is really omnipotent and needs no help to save anybody. Then, reader, be sure you utterly abandon to God and take Jesus for everything. In that case He will baptize you with the Holy Ghost and fire, and send you off singing,

"I have found a friend in Jesus. He's everything to me.
   He's the fairest of ten thousand to my soul.
The Lily of the Valley, in Him alone I see
   All I need to cleanse and make me fully whole.
Insorrow He's my comfort, in trouble He's my stay;
   He tells me every care on Him to roll.
He's the Lily of the Valley, the bright and morning Star.
   He's the fairest of ten thousand to my soul.

He all my griefs has taken, and all my sorrows born;
   In temptation He's my strong and mighty tower.
I have all for Him forsaken, and all my idols torn
   From my heart, and now He keeps me by His power.
Though all the world forsake me, and Satan tempt me sore,
   Through Jesus I shall safely reach the goal.
He's the Lily of the Valley, the bright and morning Star.
   He's the fairest of ten thousand to my soul.

He will never, never leave me, nor yet forsake me here,
    While I live by faith and do His blessed will.
A wall of fire about me, I've nothing now to fear,
    With His manna He my hungry soul shall fill.
Then sweeping up to glory, to see His blessed face,
    Where rivers of delight shall ever roll.
He's the Lily of the Valley, the bright and morning Star.
    He's the fairest of ten thousand to my soul.

Take Him for everything and you get everything, because He is everything. If you do not take Him for everything you are going to trend away into idolatry, thinking something else is necessary to your salvation. In that case you have already become an idolater, like Roman Catholics, bowing down to their images and to the pope, and even to the priest, thinking that they can give them salvation, and like Campellites, worshiping the water god, thinking immersion is necessary to salvation and not only swimming into idolatry but actually infidelity on the Holy Ghost, denying His personality, making Him an influence, even identifying Him with the written Word, which is only His breath.

The Campbellite Church is the most popular and aggressive in all this country, because it has no cross and wages no war with the sin personality, but compromises with old Adam, dresses him up, educates him, having taken him into the church and makes a preacher of him and he proves exceedingly adroit manipulating hell-hatched heresies, i. e., baptismal regeneration, to slide people into hell over the greased plank of immersion for remission; when the very word immersion is not in the Bible, nor anything of that meaning ever used to explain **baptidzo.**

(g)   There are two words which mean immersion in the New Testament: **katapontidzo,** (Matt. 18: 6), and **buthidzo,** (1 Tim. 5: 9); but neither of them ever used a single time to define **baptidzo;** showing that immerse is not a meaning to the word. Meanwhile the best lexical authorities in the world,

Dr. John Schlusner, of Germany, the very top of authority, and Dr. J. W. Robinson in America and others certify that in the sense of immerse it is never used in the New Testament. We admit that to sink like a ship in the sea is a primary meaning of the word but does not bring it up at all but leaves it down there to stay for ever. The practice of immersionists to put you down and then to lift you out, is not a meaning of the word and never was anywhere. While **baptidzo,** to baptize, is a Greek word and simply means to cleanse, purify, wash, which are all synonomous, simply meaning to purify. **Immergo,** immerse, is a pure Latin word and would be in the Latin Bible if it were ever the meaning of **baptidzo,** but as it is never used in the Latin Bible, it certainly is not the meaning of the word.

I hold in my hand the highest New Testament authority in all the world, the concensus of all the critics of Christendom, by Wescott and Hort and used as the standard of the whole Christian world. It has a New Testament lexicon and does not give immerse as a definition of **baptidzo** at all, but simply defines it, to cleanse, purify, wash.

Chapter II.

OUR SAVIOR'S DEFINITION

He constantly defines **baptidzo** by **cartharidzo,** which has no meaning but to purify. (Luke 11: 38.)

A Pharisee invites Jesus to dine with him. He walks in and sits down and proceeds to eat without washing His hands—a religious ceremony appertaining to which the Pharisees were exceedingly punctilious, as they were the holiness people of the Jewish church, but they had let the spirit evanesce and sank down into dead formality and hollow hypocrisy, so that our Savior called them whitened sepulchres externally, but internally full of dead men's bones. They proceed to criticize Him at once inwardly when He proceeded to answer them orally, "You Pharisees make clean the outside of the cup and the plate while the inside is full of polution and defilement." The word here is **catharidzo,** which has no meaning but to purify, whereas the E. V. says, "wash."

In all our Savior's ministry He constantly uses **baptidzo,** simply in the sense of purify. Therefore it is synonomous with **hagiadzo,** to sanctify. (Eph. 5: 25-27.) "Husbands love your wives as Christ loved the Church and gave Himself for her that He might sanctify her, purifying her by the washing of water through the Word, that He might present her to Himself a glorious Church having neither spot or wrinkle nor any such thing."

In this scripture we have **catharidzo** (verse 26), given as the definition of **hagiadzo,** sanctify. Here we see our Savior's definition of His Church, no denomination, nor sect, nor company of people in any way, but the children of God, having been born of the

Spirit throughout the whole world,, in all churches, denominations and sects and some of them in no denomination. They have but two experiences, the one, the supernatural birth and the other entire sanctification, wrought by the baptism which Jesus gives with the Holy Ghost and fire, i. e., He uses the Holy Ghost to purify your heart from all unrighteousness, just as the laundryman thoroughly cleanses the garments from all impurity. He is the omnipotent agent of expurgation, while the blood of which He is the custodian, is the infallible elixir of expurgation; the Holy Spirit applying it to cleanse the heart from all unrighteousness. Meanwhile the spirit is the medium through which the Holy Spirit applies the Blood. As we read and study the Word, feed on it, the Holy Spirit, the author of it, reveals it to us and opens our understanding to its deep and beautiful truth, thus using the Word as the instrument of our sanctification, the dispenser of the Blood to every avenue of the soul.

This glorious Church is not only free from every stain because the Blood washed it away, but when clothing is thoroughly laundered and every atom of impurity eliminated, it is dry, hard and stiff and would be uncomfortable to wear. Consequently this omnipotent laundryman, the Holy Ghost, runs over it His great and ponderous hot iron, removing all the wrinkles, so that the soul is without spot or wrinkles.

When the Lord gave me the wonderful baptism of the Holy Ghost and fire forty-five years ago, I was a Southern Methodist preacher, a college president, a Free Mason, an Odd Fellow and had my life insured. Therefore you see I had a heap of wrinkles, but when the Holy Ghost ran His ponderous iron over my soul, they all evanesced and I have been shouting from that day to this, so delighted with the glorious Church without spot or wrinkle.

Chapter III.

THE PROPHECY OF JOHN THE BAPTIST

The constant battle cry of this wonderful hermit prophet of the wilderness, was: "He will baptize you with the Holy Ghost and fire, whose fan is in His hand, He will thoroughly purify His threshing floor, gather His wheat into the granary and burn up the chaff with unquenchable fire." N. B. John used the word to tell them what Jesus will do for them with the Holy Ghost and fire and what he does with water. We know on the day of Pentecost the Holy Ghost and fire fell on them and baptized them. It is a burning shame for immersionists to stand up before the people and twist this into an immersion as they do, without the shadow of truth or even plausability, it is a travesty on common sense and honesty and a burlesque on the audience. It is impossible for you to reveal two opposite accounts in the use of the same word. If you give orders to two boys, one to plow the garden and the other to hoe it, you have to use two different words to get them to do separate and distinct works. The Bible is the most sensible book in the world and has no nonsense in it. It is grievous to the Holy Ghost and wicked in the sight of God to pervert it and handle it deceitfully. I have been in Jerusalem at the very time of year, early in June, when Jesus baptized them with the Holy Ghost and fire, thus inaugurating that wonderful revival, resulting in the conversion of eight thousand in one day.

Jerusalem is a mountain city, to high to dig wells, for it is above the water line.

(h) During the winter season every man catches

all the water that falls in his premises and stores it away in subterranean tanks and cisterns, but in the summer it gets so scarce that it is bought and sold. Go there now (June) and you see a man coming with a goat on his shoulder, the whole animal to all appearance, carrying it along. The goat it not there, it has been ingeniously slipped out and eaten up and the skin cunningly transformed into a water bottle.

At the time of the year when the Pentecost revival took place, water was not bought and sold in Jerusalem. The city was then supplied with water carried by an aqueduct from the pools of Solomon.

When the Lord baptized the 120 with the Holy Ghost and fire, they shouted so loudly as to arouse the multitude gathered from every nation under heaven, the great annual Pentecost on Mt. Moriah, separated from Zion by the Tyrubian Valley. They came in multitudes through curiosity to see what was the matter, crowding every street and alley and house tops and south wall of the city very near. Peter's sermon was a volcano breaking forth in full blast, roaring amid lightnings, thunders and earthquakes, with his stentorious voice, showing the multitude irrefutably from the scriptures that the Jesus of Nazareth, whom they had crucified fifty days antecedently, was none other than the Christ for whom they had waited four thousand years. Fast as those godly people saw that he was correct, the light flashed over their faces and their eyes sparkled as they shouted, "I see it! I see it! What shall I do to be saved?" Peter, replying tells them to repent and be baptized, (i. e., each one who has repented, because when a man repents God always forgives), the baptism being only for saved people and received as a confirmation of sins remitted and their acceptance of Jesus as their Christ of prophecy.

Now the Apostles scatter out everywhere preaching to the multitudes and by this time one hundred thousand. Meanwhile I trow the women with their weak voices heroically gather up the converts, so fast as they testify and baptize them, as under the Levitical law every ceremonial clean person was competent to sprinkle the water of purification on the subject of ceremonial defilement, which was their baptism. This conclusion is confirmed by the fact that the three thousand in the morning service and the five thousand in the afternoon all received baptism, while the preaching was going on, as there was not separate service for it after adjournment. If they had immersed them, they would have been at it for days and weeks immersing those eight thousand, whereas there was no immersion water nearer than the Jordan, fifty miles, and it is certain they did not go to it. The whole matter is perfectly consistant and beautiful, on the hypothesis that they had measured it in the Bible mode, affusion, sprinkling and pouring, which you find in both Testaments very frequently, whereas immersion is a stranger in the blessed Book.

(i) The Campbellites say there was no Holy Ghost baptism after the day of Pentecost and then it was only administered to the Apostles, and never will be given to anybody else, in flat contradiction of Peter. (Acts 2:39.) Having commanded them in the 38th verse, "Repent and let each one of you (who has repented) be baptized unto the remission of your sins and you shall receive the gift of the Holy Ghost," i. e., the baptism of the Holy Ghost, as He never comes in to abide in an unclean heart, and baptism has no meaning but to purify. "For the promise is unto you and your children and to all who are afar off even as many as the Lord our God shall call." Here you see that the baptism of the Holy Ghost is for all the people whom God calls with the Gospel, throughout all nations and dispensations, absolutely without restriction.

Chapter IV.

THE SYNONYMY OF BAPTISM AND SANCTIFICATION

We have this confirmed in many scriptures, i. e., the whole New Testament confirms the hypothesis that the baptism of the Holy Ghost and sanctification are one and the same work of grace. Those scriptures above given (Luke 11:38), where our Savior defines **baptidzo** (E. V., wash) by **catharidzo,** which has no meaning but to purify, i. e., to take out of you everything Satan put in you and give you a clean heart in which case the Holy Spirit always comes in to abide. Also (Eph. 5:26), where we have **hagiadzo** defined by the word **catharidzo,** (E. V.), "That He might sanctify and purify her by the washing of water through the Word." Here you see purify is used synonymously with sanctify; simply meaning to take out of us what Satan put in us. Hence the baptism of the Holy Ghost and sanctification are simply two terms for the same great work of grace. (Heb. 12:14), "Without sanctification no one shall see the Lord."

(j) (Isa. 63rd ch.): "Who art thou that comes from Edom, with dyed garment fro Bozrah? I that speak in righteousness mighty to save. * * * I have trodden the wine press alone, there was none to help. Mine own arm brought salvation to me."

These scriptures show clearly the perfect championship of our Savior, that He has no help and needs none. All this human cry of popery, prelacy and priest craft, belong to the strategy of anti-christ, who takes the place of Christ, as anti, means instead of. We have the same strategy with Campbellites and Mormons and sometimes with orthodox churches when they have grieved away the Holy Spirit and backslidden. The whole sum and substance is Satan's fantasmagoria and manipulation to lasso the people and get them to take a sustitute for Christ, who needs no help to do His work. He says in John 11 ch.: "I am the resurrection and the life." Every sinner is a spiritual corpse, till Jesus raises him from the dead. While this resurrection, which is a supernatural birth which is an absolute **sine qua non** without which every sinner must topple into hell. After this he must be expurgated from hereditary depravity, or he will grieve the Holy Spirit, his sanctifier, and make his bed in a backslider's hell. All children have to be born before they can be baptized. Therefore the baptism which Jesus gives is in its very nature the second work of grace in every case and is absolutely essential to salvation. Whereas Satan, through his preachers, the false prophets, lays earth and hell under contribution to substitute the preachers for Jesus, the water for the Holy Ghost and in that case hell will come in as a substitute for heaven, as an inevitable, logical sequence. Hence the great rally on immersion; Campbellites and Mormons making it essential to salvation, and abnegating the baptism of the Holy Ghost altogether, thus effectually substituting it for the baptism which Jesus gives with the Holy Spirit, thus adroitly switching Jesus off and putting in the Campbellite preacher and switching off the Holy Ghost and putting in water, which simply means damnation, as the Lord has the creed, without holiness no man shall see Him.

(k) The counterfeit Tongue Movement is the grandest rally Satan has made in our day to actually counterfeit the Holy Ghost, capture it and make capital of it. It came to us from the Spiritualists. When they were in full blast in Los Angeles, Sister

Ferguson told me about an old Spiritualist who had been with them thirty years and had received some awakening and was trying to get saved, but had been so long demonized that he could not make any headway. So when the Tongue Movement came thither, he went to their meetings and saw them get what they called the baptism of the Holy Ghost and heard them speak with tongues as they claimed and said to her that it was just what he had seen and heard in the seanances of the Spiritualists these thirty years.

When I was preaching in the Penial Mission in Stockton, Cal., the Sister in charge told me that a woman with whom she was well acquainted, and who had been a Spiritualist medium, had gotten converted, joined the Holiness Movement and was preaching. When the Tongue Movement came around, she went to their meeting and went to the altar to seek the gift of tongues, and when she got it; she said, "Why, that is just what I had when a Spiritualist medium."

(1) The simple fact which is well demonstrated, the the people in the Tongue Movement who receive what they call the baptism, do not get it, because the very meaning of it is to purify your heart and instead of bearing the fruits of holiness, they go the other way and backslide and often go into gross wickedness and immoralities. I have traveled more extensively among the Holiness people than any other man in the world, as I am satisfied and I have a broad opportunity to see the fruits which they bear, and am everywhere impressed that they are not the fruits of Canaan, but the bitter apples of Sodom.

Pastor Covington of Jasper Nazarene Church Ala., told me when they came into that country, their brightest and most promising young preacher joined them, received the baptism and the gift of tongues, and backslid very quickly and quit preaching and became wicked and he said that he had recently preached a whole Sunday and this young man in sight of his meeting, spent the day gambling. I many cases where they have quickly fallen into wickedness, within my personal observation till it is actually phenomenal that they backslide so quickly. And they are known to be living in wickedness at the very time they have this so-called gift of tongues as I could give many instances which is positive proof that they do not receive the baptism of the Holy Ghost, because the very meaning of baptism is to purify and nobody with a clean heart ever does commit sin, because actual sin is an effect which must proceed from a cause, and that cause is indwelling depravity. Satan had to put depravity into the hearts of Adam and Eve before he could ever get them to commit sin.

I not only have personal knowledge but especially an immense amount of information from the best Holiness people; e. g. A man in an Ohio city actually speaking with tongues in their meetings, and was drunk at the same time and actually confessed that he was drinking. I heard with my own ears a woman who claimed her baptism of the Holy Ghost and was speaking with tongues in their way in a camp-meeting in Oklahoma City and I received it from a most reliable source that she was at that time living a bad life.

(m)   When the movement first broke out I was preaching in New York City, and crossed the continent to investigate for myself, and falling in with them in Los Angeles and have been the midst of them ever since, travelling all parts of the United States and somewhat in Canada.

In the first place, I have found no instance where any of them had a tongue, as tongue simply means languages, not noises. The truth of it is, if you go to seeking anything but God, the evil spirits which throng the air (Eph. 2: 1), will come in and give you something, in order to sidetrack you and get you away from God. If they could they would give you a language, but they cannot. God alone can do that. I know languages which you know not, but I could not give you one to save my life. These evil spirits can work on your sensibilities, arousing emotions, excite you and make you jump and shout, but they cannot give you any of the graces of the Holy Spirit as they do not have them: love, joy, peace, gentleness, long-suffering, goodness, faith, meekness, holiness. They do their best to counterfeit everything God does. On the day of Pentecost the gift of ears was as prominent as that of tongues. Though the preaching was done in Greek every one heard it in his own language in which he was born. They also received real tongues, These were God's merciful miracles to expedite the launching of the Gospel Church.

Satan has made a wonderful success counterfeiting the gift of tongues and would do the same with the gift of ears if he could, but he cannot.

The reason why the Tongue people backslide so lamentably is because these evil spirits with whom they are tinkering, are all fallen angels and are of a higher order of being than we are, wiser and stronger. Therefore our security is in standing aloof, keeping our eye on Jesus, our only leader and obeying the Holy Ghost, our only guide, and walking in the light of God's Word, our only authority, as man is a trinity, consisting of spirit soul and body; the Holy Spirit leading the human spirit, the Word our immortal intellect and Providence our bodies. If we are true to this tripple leadership of the Lord, we are as sure of heaven as if we were in it.

(n)   God commands us (1 Jno. 4: 1): "Try the spirits and see if they be of God because many false prophets have gone forth into the world." How are we to try the spirits? By the Word of the Lord. Every spirit which is not in harmony with God's Word is from the bottomless pit, dressed up as an angel of light and playing off on you, in order to deceive and sidetrack you.

The Tongue Movement just simply goes down when brought to the test of God's Word. When the people are all the time wanting to know what language they have, they say it is an unknown tongue. They do not know it nor anybody else and it is an utterly unknown tongue. You have nothing to do but look in your own English Bible, 1 Corinthians, chapters 12 and 14 and you see "unknown" is italicized, which is a confession on the port of the translators that it is not in the Bible and never was I read the pure original Greek like English, using nothing else for about forty years. Therefore I know that "unknown" is not in the original and never was. The truth of the matter is, there is no unknown tongue, because tongue is a language, and there never was a language that some nation didn't speak and never will be.

(o)   Their constant battle cry is, "These signs shall follow them that believe, They shall take up serpents, if they drink any deadly poison, it shall not hurt them, they shall speak with other tongues and they shall lay hands on the sick and they shall recover."

It is a well-known fact that the last twelve verses of Mark, including the above, are not in the original and never were. Peter who dictated that Gospel and Mark who wrote it had been in heaven several hundred years before those last twelve verses were in the Bible. Mark's Gospel closes with the eighth verse. See Tischendorf's Manuscript, the Sinaitic, the oldest in the world and the only one entire.

Long after Mark and Peter had finished their

work and gone to heaven, somebody thought Mark stopped too soon and took it on himself to finish off his Gospel, rounding it after the manner of Matthew and putting in the commission which says the Gospel is to be preached to every creature in our dispensation, which would postpone the coming of the Lord, perhaps forever. Matthew gives the commission straight and clear, commanding us to preach the Gospel to every nation and the Lord says (Matt. 24: 14), that when we do that He will return. So we may rest on our Lord's own words in those two passages in Matthew, assuring us that when we preach the Gospel to every nation, He will return; whereas, the statement, "every creature," would postpone His return almost indefinitely. This trouble is all relieved by the simple fact that those last twelve verses of Mark are not in the original. Our dispensation is not to get every person evangelized, but simply to call and aquip the Bride, as you see clearly revealed in Acts 15th chapter, that our work is to take a people out of all nations for the Lord and get them ready, and He says, "After these things I will return and build again the throne of David, and the ruins of the same and set it up again, in order that the remainder of the people may seek out the Lord, even all on whom His name has been called," showing up the fact that while our work is to get the Bride ready, the on-coming millennial dispensation will get all the people saved.

The very fact that this scripture—the last twelve verses of Mark—are not in the original, relieves us of the conclusion that all who receive the baptism of the Holy Ghost manifest it by speaking with tongues.

We now leave the great trouble with the Tongue heresy, founded on the spurious passage. Early in the Holiness Movement, we had a terrible battle with the snake preachers. I frequently met them and heard them stoutly contend that you must be able to handle rattle snakes with impunity, as an evidence that you have the baptism of the Holy Ghost. If the Tongue Movement would be consistent, they would have to require the test of handling the rattlers and drinking poison, as well as speaking with tongues, because they are all laid down together; so if you take one item, you must take all. The thing to do in all matters of doubt and controversy, is to walk in the light of the Lord. During the long roll of the Dark Ages, not one man in a thousand, nor one woman in twenty thousand could read or write; meanwhile, much error got into the scriptures, many things being added; while some of the precious Word, slipping the fingers of the translators, got lost.

(p) All that dreary midnight of time, while sacerdotalism held sway, the priest who could invent most ceremonies was considered the smartest and in order to popularize the victory of the Trinitarians over the Arians, brought much corruption into the Church, such as the water god and trine immersion, which racked the Church for several centuries. Eventually truth, fortunately prevailing and trinitarianism achieving the victory over Arianism, which they impressed on all the people by their baptism, dipping the subject right side downward in the name of the Father; then raising him up and dipping him in the name of the Son, left side downward; then lifting him up faceforemost in the name of the Holy Ghost.

As the people couldn't read, these three immersions in water administered to them, were very important instructors on that important line of trinitarianism.

Dr. Dowie recently gave great notoriety to the trine immersion, in a fruitless attempt to restore it, believing that it was the Apostolic practice and terribly castigating the Baptists for their single dip, calling it Unitarian baptism.

When the Trinitarians achieved the victory over the Unitarians, they inserted the three heavenly witnesses in John's first epistle, (1 John 5: 7), which is not in the original. During that long, dark period in which Satan's trinity—sin, ignorance and superstition—captured the Church, and so much error got into the Bible, both on the line of addition, bringing in many interplations, and subtraction, transcribers inadvertently permitting words and phrases to slip through their fingers and get lost. Fortunately all this time God had the precious Word safe in the Convent of St. Catherine on Mt. Sinai, where He first revealed it to Moses, 3580 years ago. In His own good time, in 1859, He miraculously revealed it to His faithful servant Tishendorf, after he had hunted forty years for everything that would throw light on the Bible. He was lingering in an old closet in that venerable convent which was built in the second century to commemorate the giving of the law, contemplating quite a lot of old parchment rolls, so ancient that no human eye could see a letter to save his life. Eventually his intention spontaneously focalized on one of the largest and apparently most ancient and seemed to linger on it, having no inclination to look away, but wrapped more and more diagnosis, when God spoke to him from heaven as He did to Moses 3500 years antecedently; in a still small voice, as He did to Elijah in the cave on the same mountain at a subsequent date, distinctly articulating, "This is Mine."

(q) He then proceeds to buy it from the monks in charge of the convent, but they all shook their heads, certifying that it could not go for love or money. In the providence of God Emperor William of Germany was raised to defray all the expenses of Tischendorf all the forty years, which were great, because he frequently had groups of men hired in the ruins of ancient cities and hunting everything that they could to throw light on the precious Word.

He remembered the maxim, "Every man has his price," and began to bid, using higher and higher, till they could resist the temptation no longer, and acquiesced, receiving the princely sum of money and delivering the parchment. Tischendorf takes it in his arms and returns to Germany after an absence of forty years; delivers it to those shrewd chemists, who subject it to their powerful alkiline solutions, whose normal effect is to interpenetrate and soften it, so that they can unroll it. It is a great roll of sheep skins, having been elegantly dressed, superscribed and rolled up. Another effect of the chemicals is to bring out the old writings and render it gloriously legible and decipherable. What is it? Oh, it is a complete copy of the New Testament, dating far back into the Apostolic Age and pouring floods of light on the precious Word, as it antedated all the interpelations and eliminations, giving us the precious infallible Word, pure from the Apostolic pen.

When the venerable German prophet sees it, like old Simeon who waited in the temple for the coming of the Lord a hundred years, till they brought the infant Christ into the temple to dedicate Him, and the Holy Ghost revealed Him, and taking Him in his withered arms, died of joy, so Tischendorf, like him, his life work done, his thrilling prophetical anticipations realized, is too happy to live, God lets him go to heaven.

(r) His good providence sent to me all the way from Germany, that wonderful book which I proceeded to read in our great meetings from the Atlantic to the Pacific. The saints listening spellbound, as the sawyers on which they had been stranded evanesced, as all the pestilential heresies that swept the world with their withering sirocos, are founded on wrong translations and interpelations and deduced from eliminations. Therefore I

have nothing to do but just read the precious Word
in the pure original and those perplexing and peri-
lous heresies, spontaneously evanesce.

Consequently they clamored for me to translate
it. I hesitated, recoiling from the labor and respon-
sibility. Finally at the close of the last Camp-meeting Brother Knapp ever attended on earth, when I
bade him adieu for a midnight train, he begged me
hard to translate the New Testament into English,
offering me a thousand dollars for the work.

As the Lord had not yet told me to do it, I simply
responded, "I will, D. V." "Ask Him about it." When
I had bid him adieu, he gripped my hand, like a
drowning man, observing, "Brother Godbey, I am
never going to let go your hand till you make me two
promises, the one that you will attend my camp-
meeting, the Lord willing, as long as you live, and
the other that you will translate the New Testament out of Greek into English and go at it without
delay. I knew then that God was in it and that He
took that method of revealing to me that it was His
will and He used Brother Knapp to tell me.

Then I acquiesced, at the same time saying to
him, "You can keep your thousand dollars. Jesus
came all the way from heaven to translate me and I
would be a shabby disciple if I could not translate
His precious Word for His sake alone." Then I
went home and entered upon the work without delay
and when in the middle of the job, the telegram
came, calling me to preach his funeral, as the Lord
had translated him.

(s) "What does our Savior say about signs?
They frequently demand of Him signs from heaven."
Hear His response, "A wicked and adulterous generation seeketh after a sign, but no sign shall be given,
except the sign of the prophet Jonah, as he was a
sign to Ninevah, so the Son of man will be a sign to
this generation." (He was when risen from the

dead.)   How strange people are paradoxically gullible, seeking after signs, when Jesus pronounces sign-seekers a wicked and adulterous generation and of course on their way to hell.

The Tongue people in that way get them to pile the altar and seek the gift of tongues as a sign of the baptism of the Holy Ghost, when they have no tongue at all, because a tongue is a language and they have nothing but simply noises like frogs and birds.   The simple fact is that these demons whom they are worshiping cannot give you a language but they can stir up your emotions and arouse your sensibilities and make you jump and shout like Satan's people in saloons, circuses, race tracks, rooster fights, dog fights and all sorts of fandangoes, but they cannot give any of the graces of the Holy Spirit.   They go hundreds of miles and spend months and years seeking these signs, recklessly in the face of the infallible Teacher, who consigns to hell all sign-seekers, pronouncing them a wicked and adulterous generation.

If you have the baptism of the Holy Ghost, you do not need a sign.   It flashes from your physiognomy, echoes from your tread, and manipulates in all your handiwork.   Your whole life is a luminous panorama of the mighty work wrought in you by the blessed indwelling Holy Ghost.   How strange that highly cultured people, amid the blaze of glorious Christian civilization, prove so exceedingly humbugable.

Chapter V.

PENTECOST

The Tongue people say there was no sanctification on the day of Pentecost and that the Apostles were all sanctified when the Lord breathed on them the evening of the resurrection and said, "Receive ye the Holy Ghost." That was not their sanctification, but their reclamation. At the Last Supper Jesus said to them, You will all be offended in Me this night," i. e., backslide, which is the meaning of **scandalidzo** and has no other meaning in the New Testament.

People generally think that Peter was the only backslider. He was the most respectable in the crowd, because when they came to Jesus to arrest Him, he drew his sword and went right in to defend Him and would have fought that whole army if Jesus had let him, while the other nine skedadled away up Mt. Olivet and returned no more till after the crucifixion. John having fled away in his night apparel, the soldiers running after him to catch him and got so close on him that he jumped out of his coat, leaving it in their hands, running away in a state of nudity to the house of Rabiamos, where procuring and putting on the robe of a Jewish priest, he returned and, though known to Caiphas, as the original reveals, a kin to him, and he did not diverge on his nephew. Consequently falling in with Jesus, the soldiers, thinking he was priest, he walked by His side to the tribunal of Annas; thence to the bar of Caiphas, and thence to the Sanhedrin and thence to Pilate's judgment hall and thence to Herod's tribunal, and back to Pilate, then up rugged Calvary, where He is nailed to the cross; John sticking to Him all the while, though Peter had already denied

Him and utterly fallen and the other nine having forsaken Him in Gethsemane. Their faith there received an awful blow as if smitten by a battering ram. While looking on the bloody scene of Calvary, a mile distant across the valley of Jehosophat, their faith gradually evanesced one by one, John by His side, holding out, the last of all to give up His Christhood, but still looking for Him to revive, come down from the cross, miraculously defeat all His enemies and live on. Thus he holds on and expects Him to revive till Phillipus comes along and plunges his cruel spear into His heart and tears it to pieces. Then history (Ingraham) says "he fainted," falling on the ground because his faith in His Christhood utterly evanesced and giving up His Christhood, he dropped Him down to the plane of the prophets.

(u) Jesus three times over told them positively about His tragical end: arrested, mocked, spit upon, buffeted, scourged and crucified. Yet they did not understand it. Why? Because, as the Word says, "The Holy Ghost hid it from them. Why reveal it and then hide it so that they would never understand it?

It was indispensible that it should be revealed, because the faith of all generations rests on the prophecies. Therefore the curriculum must be complete.

Why then did the Holy Ghost conceal it from them? Because if His disciples had known that they were going to kill Him, there would have been the biggest war you ever saw, in His defence because He had filled the whole country with His miracles, healing everybody of all diseases, however terrible and incurable, till ailments and all sorts of bodily affliction had actually evanesced out of the country, as His name went to the ends of the earth and the people far and near brought their friends to be healed. Consequently every apostle was a returned recruiting officer. Peter would have been commander in chief and, brave as Napoleon Bonaparte, the people would have rallied from the ends of the earth, fought, bled and died to deliver Him from His enemies. He had come into the world to suffer and die to redeem all from death and hell. Therefore He did not want anybody to die to save His life. His apostles were all settled in the conclusion that He was truly the Christ, but believed that the Christ was immortal and could not be killed, but "would sit down on the throne of David and rule over the house of Jacob forever." (Luke 1: 34.) They did not descriminate between His two advents and understand how He came the first time to suffer and die, but will come the second time to conquer and reign forever. Therefore when they saw them killing Him, every one gave up His Christhood and dropped Him down to the plane of the prophets; but as a prophet cannot save anybody, there they all backslid in Him.

(v)   You see it in the case of the two traveling to Emmaus on the afternoon of His resurrection, when falling in with them, dropping an eclipse over their eyes, so that they did not know Him, and asking them, "What is the news?" and they say, "Are you but a stranger in Jerusalem and not posted in the news?" "Oh, what news?" "Why, concerning Jesus of Nazareth, a man, a prophet, and we were hoping that He were the one to redeem Israel, but our rulers have delivered Him up and they have crucified Him." You see here they did not call Him the Christ, but a prophet, and though they were hoping that He would redeem Israel, they had given it all up and settled down in the conclusion that He was only a prophet; still believing sanguinely that He was the greatest prophet who had ever lived on the earth, because He had wrought more miracles and greater than any of the prophets.

Therefore going on till they turn in for lodging and constraining Him, though a stranger, to stop and enjoy their kind hospitality. When at the supper table He reveals Himself to them, breaking bread as He had done so much during His ministry, then their eyes were opened and they recognized Him at once and He vanished out of their sight. The rapture of their spirits supercedes their physical hunger and they at once run back to Jerusalem and find all of their comrades shut up in a room for fear of the Jews and relate their thrilling story, when He at once stands in their midst, ringing in their ears, "Peace be unto you," and going round breathing on them with the benediction, "Receive ye the Holy Ghost."

The Tongue people conclude that He sanctified them then, and consequently they did not receive it at Pentecost, but the baptism of the Holy Ghost.

N. B. The Holy Ghost is the executive of the Trinity and it is fanatical to conclude that we only receive Him in sanctification. In conviction we receive Him as a Convictor; in regeneration we receive Him as a Regenerator; in reclamation we receive Him as a Restorer; in sanctification we receive Him as a Sanctifier and an indwelling Comforter; in glorification we receive Him as a Perfector from all the infirmities superinduced by the fall.

Pentecost is so-called because that word means fifty and it occured just fifty days after the Passover and it was instituted to commemorate the giving of the Law. As the Law says, "The soul that sinneth, it shall die," (Ezek. 18: 4, 20), therefore our pentecost is the execution of the criminal in every human heart, i. e., the old man of sin. Therefore you must have your pentecost which is the baptism of the Holy Ghost, administrated so copiously by our Savior on that great and notable day when He

verified the prayer of one hundred and twenty which
they had been sending up those solid ten days,

> "Refining fire, go through my heart;
>   Illuminate my soul;
> Scatter thy fire through every part,
>   And sanctify the whole.
>
> "Oh that He now from heaven might fall,
>   And all my sins consume!
> Come, Holy Ghost, for Thee I call;
>   Spirit of burning, come!"

(x)   The Tongue people are awfully erratic bringing in the baptism of the Holy Ghost as a third blessing, from the simple fact that baptism and sanctification are precisely synonomous, one and the same
thing, designating the same great and glorious work
of grace.   This is demonstrated by our Savior's con-
scious use of them interchangeably.   The Bible
would be very monotonous if you should use the
same word all the time for each one of the mighty
works of grace involved in the great plan of salvation,
i. e., regeneration and sanctification.   For the former
we have conversion, born from above, reconciliation,
salvation, and some other words, perhaps all designating the first great work wrought in the heart,
designated by justification, denotative of the can-
cellation of our sins from heaven's chancellory, and
regeneration, which means the creation of the divine life in the dead soul. While the second work of
grace is revealed by the word sanctification, holiness,
perfection, the baptism of the Holy Ghost, full re-
newal, etc., all of which denote the same great and
glorious work—the crucifixion of the old man and
the infilling of the heart with the blessed Holy Spirit
coming in to abide.

(y)   A mistake is made by the Holiness people
concerning the baptism of the Holy Ghost to be simply an impulsive blessing and the infilling of the

Spirit, whereas the uniform definition of it given by our Savior, especially as well as the apostles, is simply a purification which is the only meaning of **catharidzo**, which is currently in the New Testament as a definition of **baptidzo**. (Luke 11: 38; Eph. 5: 26.) "For the sake of these I sanctify Myself in order that they may be sanctified through the truth." (John 17: 18.) Isaiah says, "Thou hast laid on Him the iniquity of us all." While He was dying on the cross, He cried out, "My God, why hast Thou forsaken Me?" I trow at that notable epoch, God laid on Him all the sins that had ever been committed or ever would be or all the inbred sin that had ever been inherited or ever would be. All the sins of ignorance and the oceans of infirmities. And consequently turned His face away as He could not look upon sin, even on His Son.

Having thus taken all the sins of Adam's ruined race on His spotless soul, He climbs the rugged cross and there expiates them all, i. e., legalistically buries them all in the Fountain filled with Blood, i. e., in that magnitudinous sepulchre, the vicarious substitutionary atonement, so gloriously expurgated them as to preclude the necessity for a solitary soul to sink into hell.

Our Savior calls all of His sufferings a baptism: "I have a baptism to be baptized with," because His sufferings legalistically expurgated the sins of the whole world, throwing wide open the door for every human soul to walk in His footprints to the cross and let the Holy Ghost nail him to it, till he bleeds and dies.

Hence we see that the great mediatorial work of Christ to redeem the world by His expiatory sufferings, His all-denominated baptism in perfect harmony with the definition of the word **catharidzo**, which is used thousands of times in the Bible with no other meaning but purify. Those innumerable catharisms performed by the priests in the temple were all ceremonial purifications. In their succession we have water baptism, which is simply a ceremonial purification wrought in the heart by the Holy Spirit, when Jesus baptizes you, thus crucifying the old man and destroying the body of sin and making your heart clean. God bless you all.

Dr. W. B. Godbey.